BILL FRISELL

AN ANTHOLOGY

Photo by Luciano Viti

Cover design by Gwen Terpstra
Drawings by Bill Frisell

ISBN 1-57560-412-4

Visit our website at www.cherrylane.com

PREFACE

I'm really excited to have this collection of music together for the first time. This is certainly not all I've written, but hopefully it gives a pretty good cross section of what I've been doing over the past 20 years or so, starting with one of the first tunes I ever wrote ("Throughout") all the way up to the most recent ("Blues Dream").

I'd rather not try to explain too much about how any of this music might be approached, but let the notes speak for themselves. I don't know who it was that said "Talking about music is like dancing about architecture." When I've played these pieces over the years with my various groups, they've been a jumping-off place—hopefully with something new happening each time. There's no real set way to approach them. I hope that anyone else playing them will try to find her own way—changing the tempo, orchestration, whatever. Included in the book is a discography so, if you're interested, you can listen to what the pieces sounded like at the particular moment they were recorded—but they're not really meant to be played "just like the record."

One of my heroes, Thelonious Monk, created a whole world in his compositions. They are usually associated with the piano, but could be orchestrated in so many other ways. I hope the music in this book will be of interest not only to guitar players. Some of it was written with the guitar in mind, but much of it is presented like a score and could be arranged in any number of ways, for any instrument(s).

When I was at the Berklee College of Music in the early '70s, I studied arranging and composition with some incredible teachers: Herb Pomeroy and Mike Gibbs. Most of what we did there was centered around big band writing. I was gathering valuable information but didn't feel like I was writing anything at the time that had its own voice. I just wanted to play the guitar and was trying to accumulate as much as I could and apply it to my instrument. I often wish I could go back and take those classes again.

Slowly over the years, my motives for writing have changed. I'm still a "guitar player" but the writing has become much more than a way of adding to my guitar vocabulary. I'm trying to find a "world" or context in which to put my instrument (and the musicians I'm playing with), to give us something to say.

Many times when I pick up the guitar, it feels like it's for the first time all over again. Music is very humbling. Writing is the same—sometimes it feels like I'm just writing the same song over and over again. Someone once said we each have only one song.

I'm not sure how writing happens—all I know is, there are no short cuts, no easy ways out. One time I was whining to my friend Wayne Horvitz, "How do you write? What should I do?" He gave me a pencil sharpener. I learned a lot from that. There's no substitute for just sitting there with your pencil and doing the work.

I've heard it said that writing is like improvising slowed down. This idea has helped me in trying to make the transition from being an improvising guitar player to a writer. When you're composing you have the chance to edit and change things, ponder over them—which can be a blessing and a curse. When do you stop? It's real easy to work it too much, so that you lose the initial inspiration and end up with nothing; on the other hand, this process might lead you on to something completely new and better than what you started with. It's hard to know when to stop.

I'm not a fisherman, but writing for me is something like what I imagine fishing to be. There's this huge ocean of music surrounding us, moving by us all the time, and if we're patient, quiet, and sit there long enough, a melody will come along. I read recently an interview with Wayne Shorter (another of my all-time favorite musician/composers). He was asked if he felt the music flowed through him. He said "No, we flow through the music." It's all around us. Another very interesting thing he said was that the best way to learn how to write is to read—read stories; you have to learn how to tell a story. The music should tell a story.

I've learned so much and been inspired by so much music. The songs of Hank Williams and Bob Dylan, Bach's violin sonatas and partitas, all the great standards and the way Charlie Parker, Sonny Rollins, Miles Davis played them. Stravinsky, Blind Willie Johnson, Burt Bacharach, Ali Farka Toure, Ravi Shankar, Dolly Parton, Aretha Franklin, Roscoe Holcomb, Charles Ives, Bernard Hermann, Aaron Copland—this list could go on for pages and pages. It's very humbling to look at the names of these masters and realize how far there is to go. I haven't even scratched the surface. It seems as though I've only just begun writing and haven't even started to figure it out and here's this big pile of music that is this book. Where did it all come from?

I'd like to thank all the musicians I've had the opportunity to play these tunes with, especially Kermit Driscoll, Joey Baron, and Hank Roberts, who played many of these when they first came about, brought life to them, and gave me the confidence to keep writing. I was playing music with Kermit long before I had written anything. He was around for my first attempts and always had so much enthusiasm. I'm so lucky to have friends like these.

Thanks so much to Hans Wendl for having the idea to do this book in the first place, for believing in the music and for his perseverance in getting it to actually happen. Thanks so much also to everybody at Cherry Lane Music for their great attention to all the details, and for letting us do it exactly the way we wanted to. Thanks to Gwen Terpstra for her always-beautiful design work, Adam Levy, Martin Lane, Lee Townsend, and Nonesuch Records.

—Bill Frisell, September 2000

Notes on "Hard Plains Drifter" or "As I take my last breath and the noose grows tight, the incredible events of the past three days flash before my eyes." (page 28)

This piece came about as a collaboration with John Zorn and my quartet (Hank Roberts, cello; Kermit Driscoll, bass; Joey Baron, drums). I gave John little bits of music that I'd written, some of them almost completed tunes and some just little phrases. He took these and, combined with his own ideas about improvised sections, rhythmic feels, and key centers, organized them all into this piece. The whole process was inspiring and we all learned a lot. It really stretched the possibilities of what we could do as a group and affected everything we were to do later. I am grateful to John for this experience. The so-called "written" music came from me, but with John's input the line between what is composed, written, arranged, or improvised becomes very blurred here. I really think of this as John Zorn's composition. The recording was arranged and produced by him. After the piece was recorded, I wrote out this chart so we could play it on gigs.

CONTENTS

IN LINE (1983)
Throughout (Version 1) 6
Throughout (Version 2) 7

RAMBLER (1985)
Music I Heard 8
Rambler 9
Resistor 10
Strange Meeting (Version 1) 12
When We Go 14

VERNON REID & BILL FRISELL:
SMASH & SCATTERATION (1986)
Amarillo Barbados 15

POWER TOOLS: STRANGE MEETING (1987)
Unscientific Americans 16

MARC JOHNSON: SECOND SIGHT (1987)
1951 18

LOOKOUT FOR HOPE (1988)
Lookout for Hope 17
Hangdog 20
Lonesome 22

BEFORE WE WERE BORN (1989)
Freddy's Step 24
Pip Squeak 26
Goodbye 27
Hard Plains Drifter 28

IS THAT YOU? (1990)
Rag 32
The Way Home 33
Twenty Years 34
Hello Nellie 38
Hope and Fear 37

WHERE IN THE WORLD? (1991)
Unsung Heroes 40
Rob Roy 42
Child at Heart 44
Beautiful E 46
Again 48
Where in the World? 50
Let Me In 53

THIS LAND (1994)
Strange Meeting (Version 2) 56
Jimmy Carter, Part 1 58
Jimmy Carter, Part 2 60
This Land 57
Monica Jane 63
Julius Hemphill 64

ELVIS COSTELLO & BILL FRISELL: DEEP DEAD BLUE (1995)
Deep Dead Blue 66

QUARTET (1996)

Tales from the Farside 68
Stand Up, Sit Down 65
Egg Radio 70
The Bacon Bunch 71
The Gallows 72
Coffaro's Theme 73

NASHVILLE (1997)

Gimme a Holler 74
Mr. Memory 75
Brother 76
Keep Your Eyes Open 78
Family (Version 1) 79
Family (Version 2) 80
We're Not from Around Here 82

GONE, JUST LIKE A TRAIN (1998)

Blues for Los Angeles 84
Verona 83
Girl Asks Boy, Part 1 86
Pleased to Meet You 88
Nature's Symphony 89
Sherlock, Jr. 92
Gone, Just Like a Train 93
The Wife and Kid 94

GOOD DOG, HAPPY MAN (1999)

Roscoe 95
Big Shoe 96
My Buffalo Girl 97
Cadillac 1959 98
The Pioneers 100
Cold, Cold Ground 101
That Was Then 102
Monroe 103
Good Dog, Happy Man 104
Poem for Eva 105
Rain, Rain 106

GHOST TOWN (2000)

Tell Your Ma, Tell Your Pa 108
Variation on a Theme (Tales from the Farside) 110
What a World 107
Big Bob 112
Winter Always Turns to Spring 114
Justice and Honor 115
Fingers Snappin' and Toes Tappin' 116

BLUES DREAM (2001)

Blues Dream 117
Ron Carter 118
Pretty Flowers Were Made for Blooming 120
Pretty Stars Were Made to Shine 117
Where Do We Go? 121
What Do We Do? 122
Dream On 123

Bill Frisell—A Timeline 124

Selected Discography 126

Index: Alphabetical List of Song Titles 127

Throughout
(Version 1)

Music by Bill Frisell

Throughout
(Version 2)

Music by Bill Frisell

Music I Heard

Music by Bill Frisell

March tempo

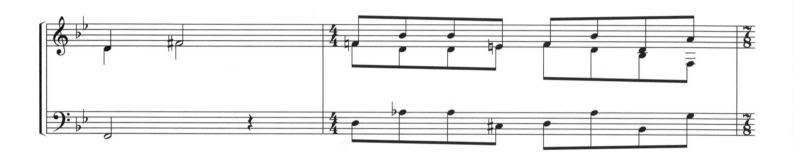

Rambler

Music by Bill Frisell

Resistor

Music by Bill Frisell

Fast Blues

* On D.C., additional voice
  plays melody of section B.

Half time

Strange Meeting
(Version 1)

Music by Bill Frisell

Medium tempo

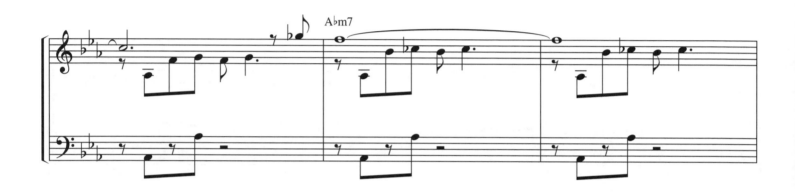

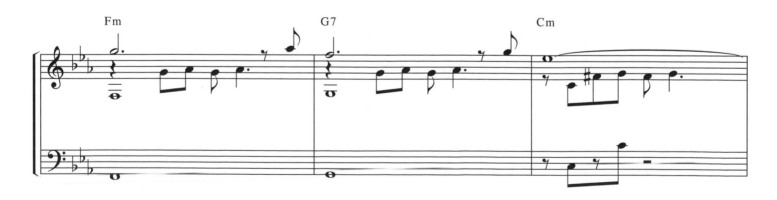

When We Go

Music by Bill Frisell

Amarillo Barbados

Music by Bill Frisell

Unscientific Americans

Music by Bill Frisell

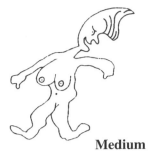

Lookout for Hope

Music by Bill Frisell

Medium tempo

1951

Music by Bill Frisell

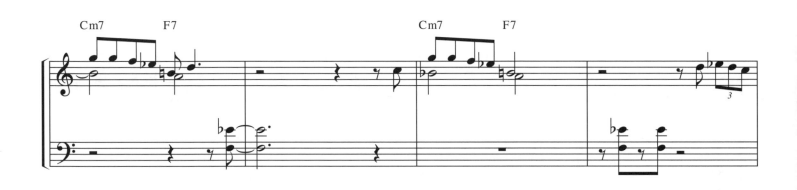

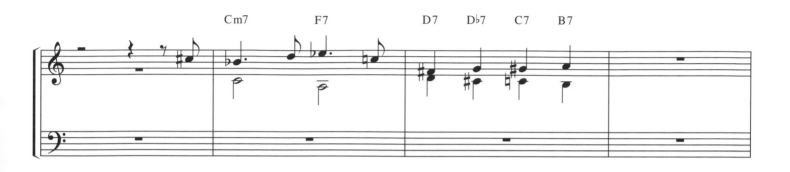

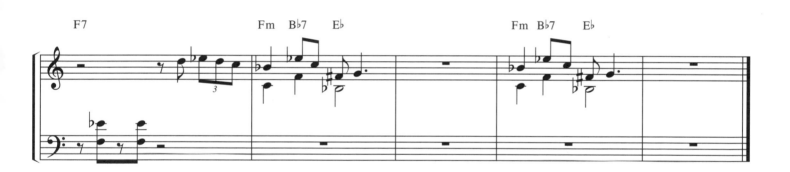

Hangdog

Music by Bill Frisell

Moderately fast

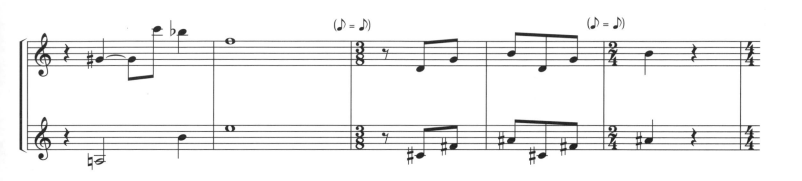

Lonesome

Music by Bill Frisell

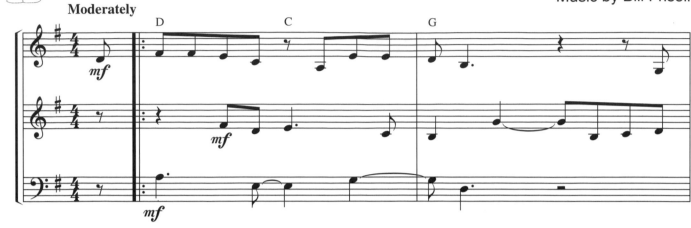

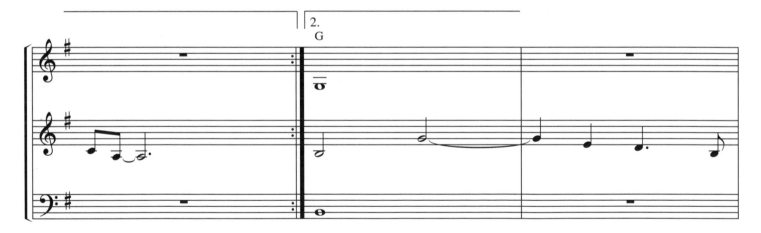

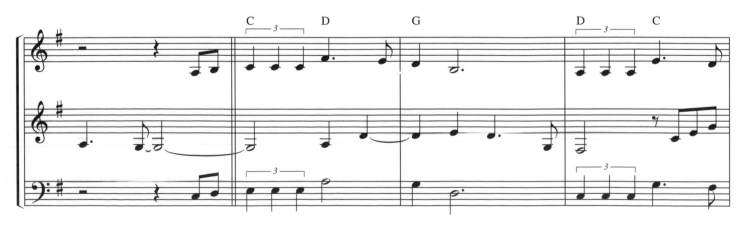

23

Freddy's Step

Music by Bill Frisell

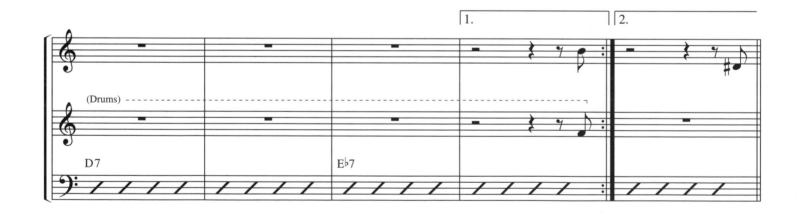

Pip Squeak

Music by Bill Frisell

Moderately fast

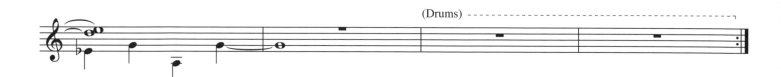

(Drums) ---

D.C.

Slower

Goodbye

Music by Bill Frisell

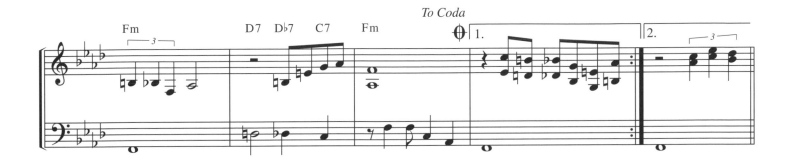

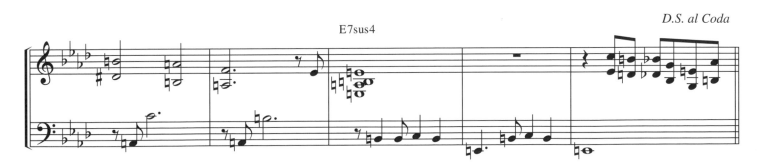

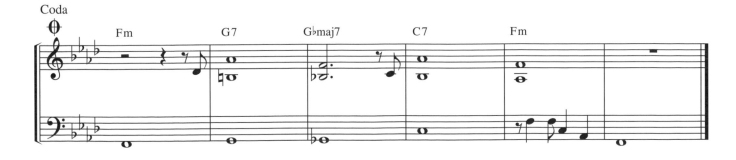

Note: On the score, the initials B, H, K, and J refer to Bill Frisell, Hank Roberts, Kermit Driscoll, and Joey Baron, and are used to indicate who should be playing at any given time.

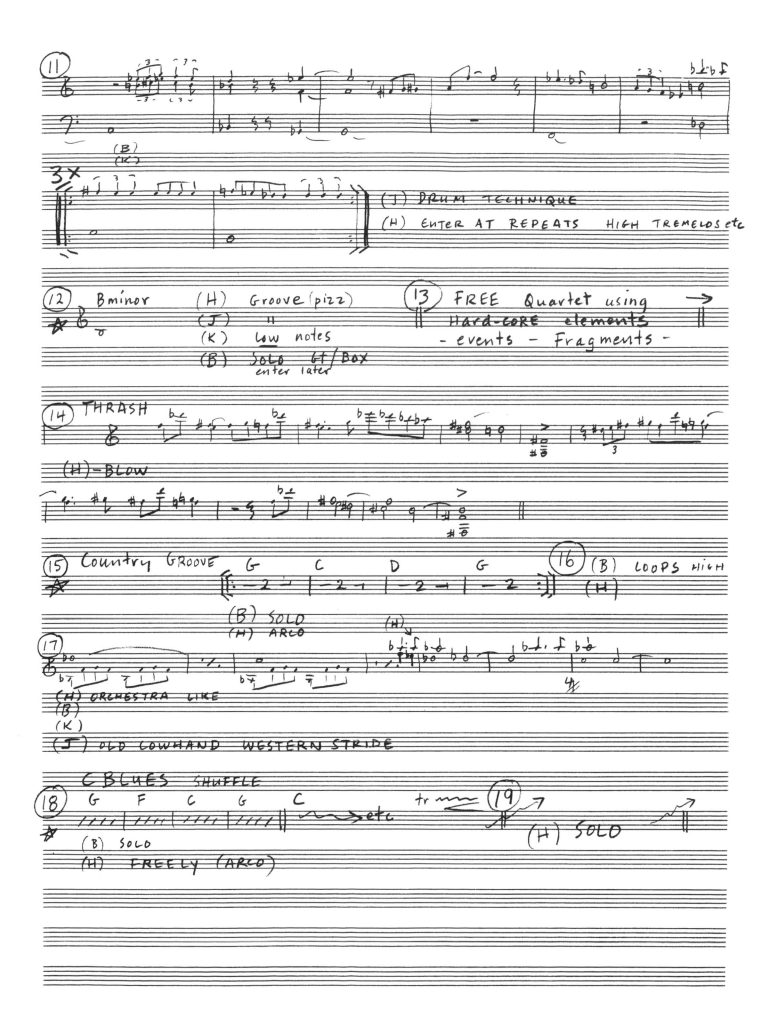

Rag

Music by Bill Frisell

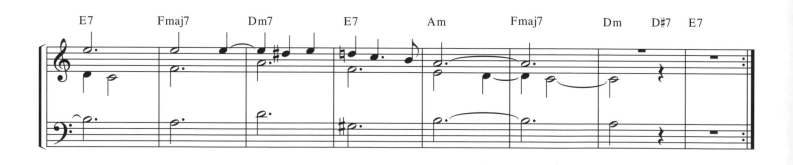

The Way Home

Music by Bill Frisell

Moderately slow

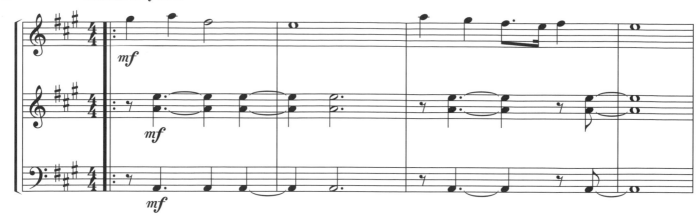

Optional Harmony

Twenty Years

Music by Bill Frisell

Hope and Fear

Music by Bill Frisell

Hello Nellie

Music by Bill Frisell

Unsung Heroes

Music by Bill Frisell

Rob Roy

Music by Bill Frisell

43

Child at Heart

Music by Bill Frisell

Medium tempo

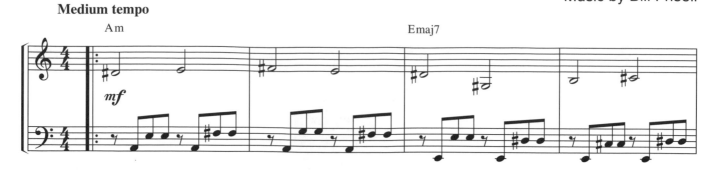

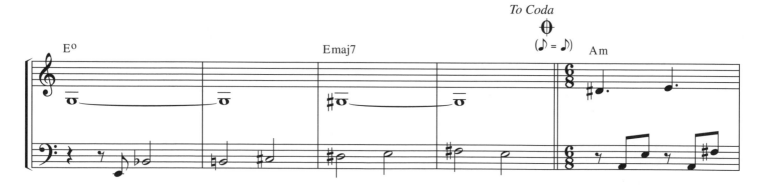

45

Beautiful E

Music by Bill Frisell

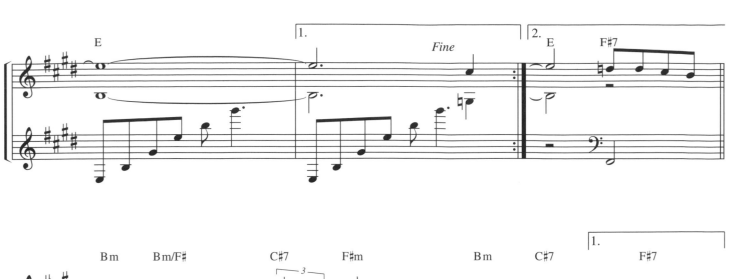

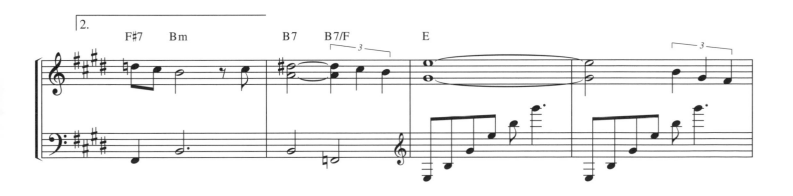

Again

Music by Bill Frisell

Medium tempo

49

Where in the World?

Music by Bill Frisell

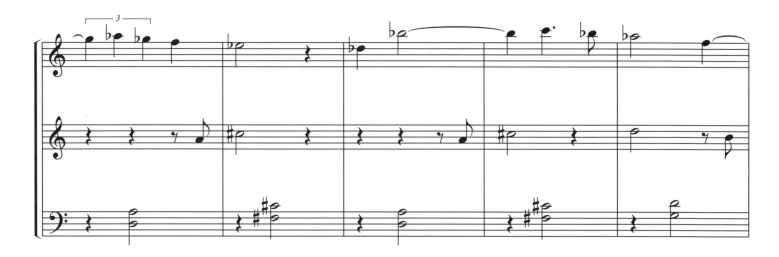

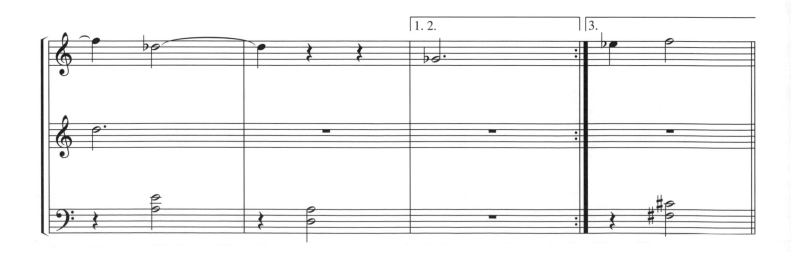

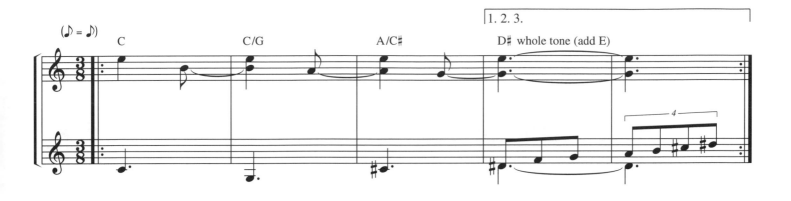

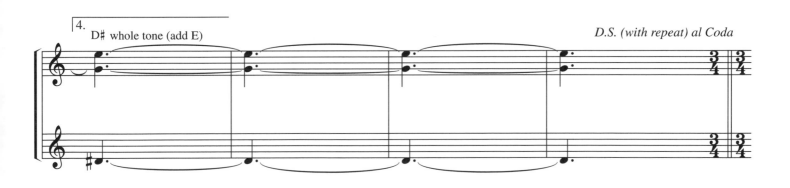

Repeat and fade

Let Me In

Music by Bill Frisell

Slowly

Play 4 times

Add low C♯ drone from here till end.

54

Strange Meeting
(Version 2)

Music by Bill Frisell

This Land

Music by Bill Frisell

Jimmy Carter, Part 1

Music by Bill Frisell

Slowly

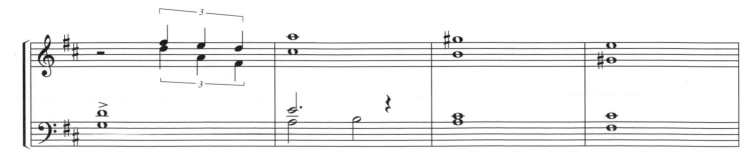

Jimmy Carter, Part 2

Music by Bill Frisell

Medium tempo

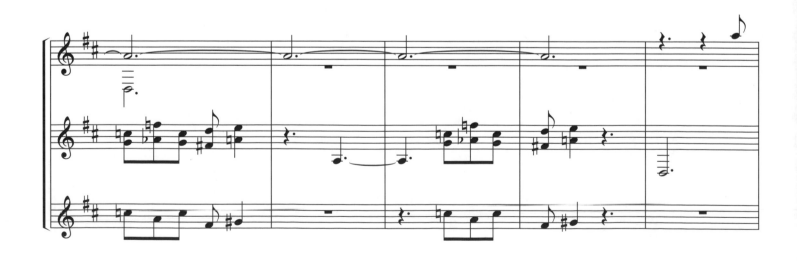

To Coda

D.S. al Coda

Coda

Monica Jane

Music by Bill Frisell

Julius Hemphill

Music by Bill Frisell

Stand Up, Sit Down

Music by Bill Frisell

Deep Dead Blue

Music by
Bill Frisell and Elvis Costello

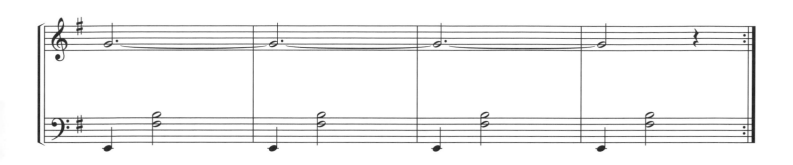

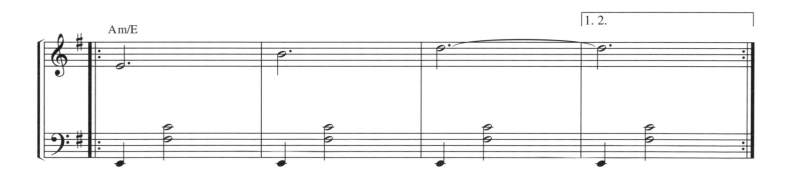

Tales from the Farside

Music by Bill Frisell

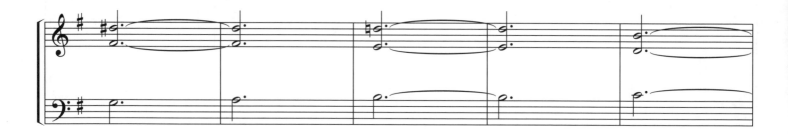

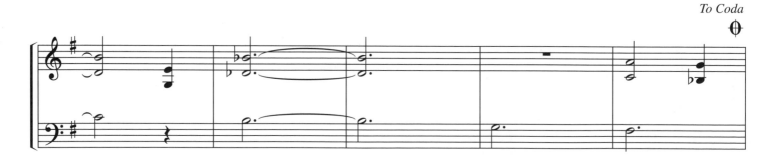

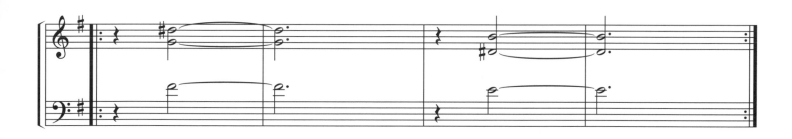

2nd time,
D.S. (with repeat) al Coda

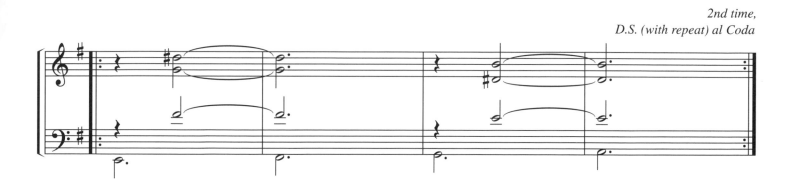

Coda

Repeat and fade

Egg Radio

Music by Bill Frisell

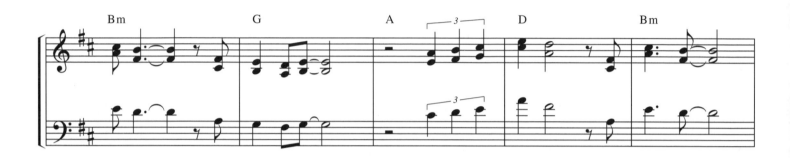

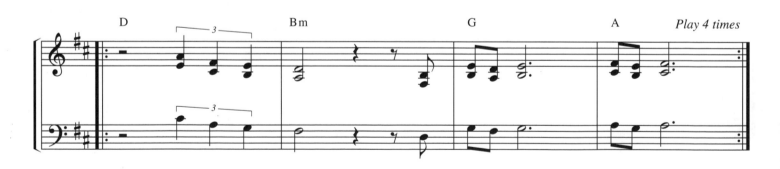

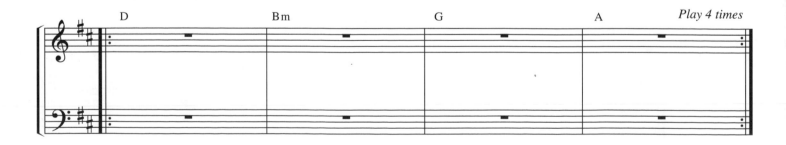

The Bacon Bunch

Music by Bill Frisell

Moderately fast March

The Gallows

Music by Bill Frisell

Coffaro's Theme

Music by Bill Frisell

Gimme a Holler

Music by Bill Frisell

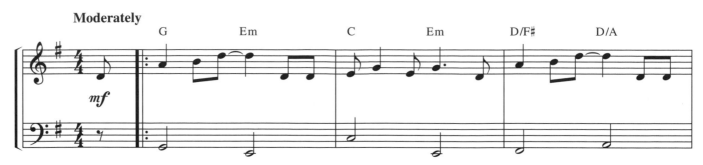

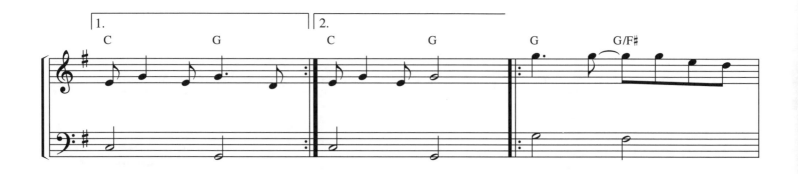

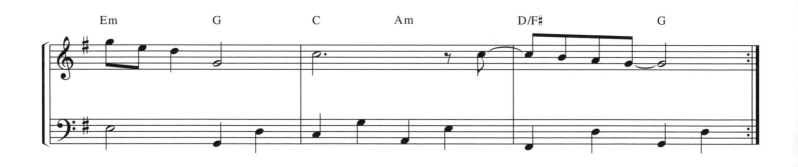

Mr. Memory

Music by Bill Frisell

Brother

Music by Bill Frisell

2nd time, D.C. (no repeat) al Fine

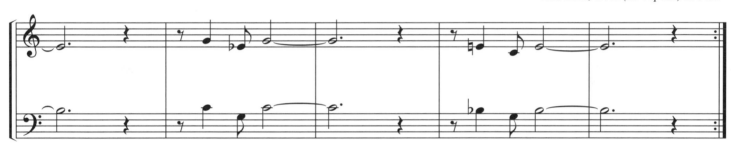

Keep Your Eyes Open

Music by Bill Frisell

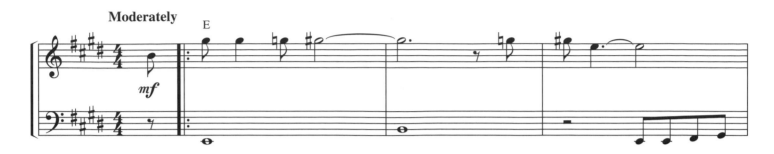

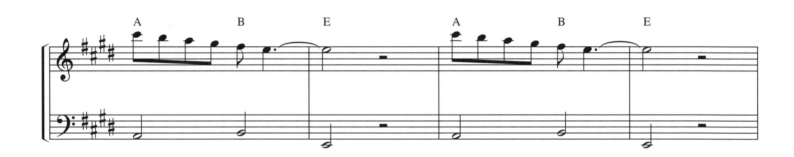

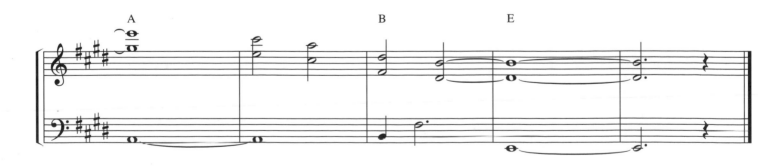

Family
(Version 1)

Music by Bill Frisell

Family
(Version 2)

Music by Bill Frisell

Medium tempo

81

We're Not from Around Here

Music by Bill Frisell

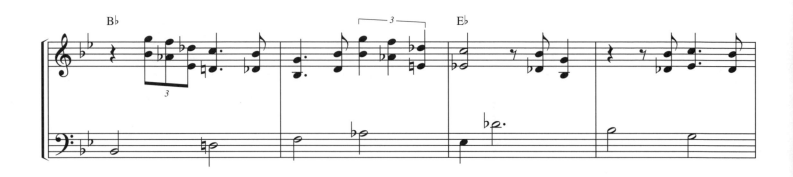

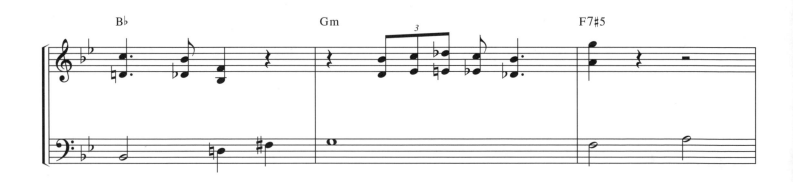

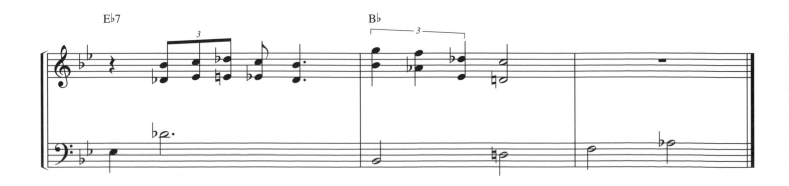

Verona

Music by Bill Frisell

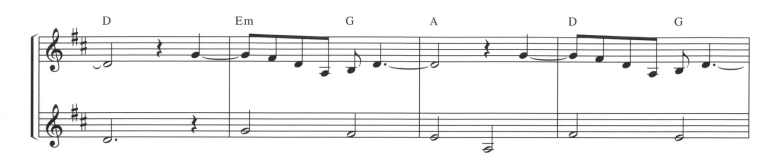

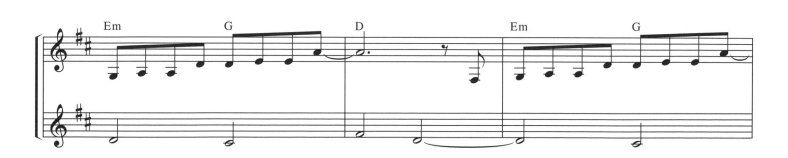

Blues for Los Angeles

Music by Bill Frisell

Medium tempo

Intro

85

Girl Asks Boy, Part 1

Music by Bill Frisell

rit.

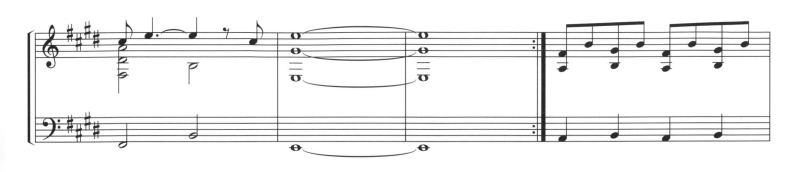

Faster tempo

Repeat and fade

Pleased to Meet You

Music by Bill Frisell

Medium tempo

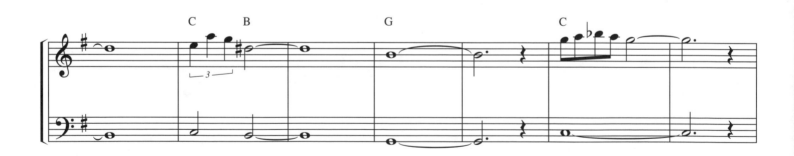

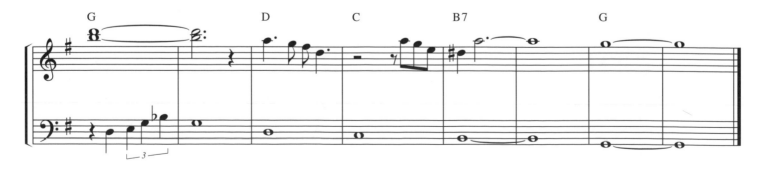

Nature's Symphony

Music by Bill Frisell

Slowly, freely

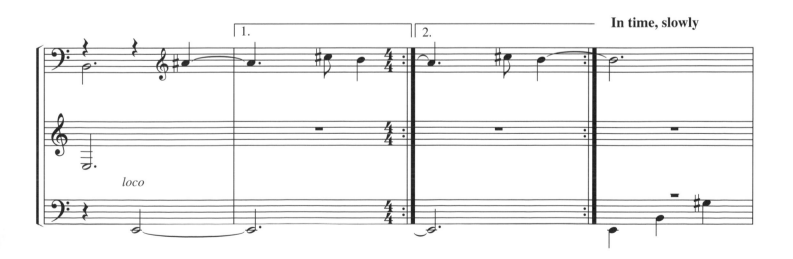

Sherlock, Jr.

Music by Bill Frisell

Gone, Just Like a Train

Music by Bill Frisell

The Wife and Kid

Music by Bill Frisell

Roscoe

Music by Bill Frisell

Big Shoe

Music by Bill Frisell

Moderately fast

My Buffalo Girl

Music by Bill Frisell

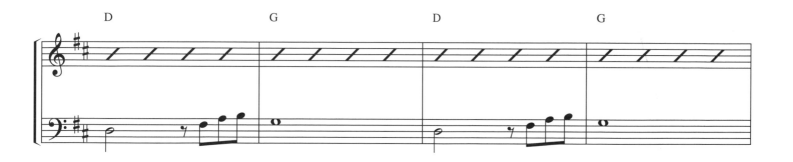

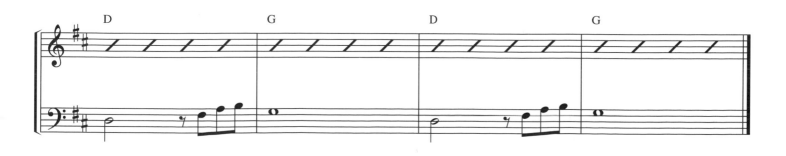

Cadillac 1959

Music by Bill Frisell

The Pioneers

Music by Bill Frisell

Cold, Cold Ground

Music by Bill Frisell

Medium tempo

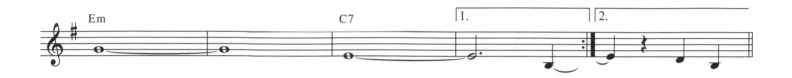

2nd time, D.C. (with repeats) al Fine

*On D.C., substitute Vamp for chords.

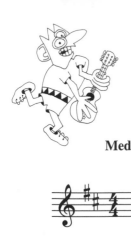

That Was Then

Music by Bill Frisell

Medium tempo

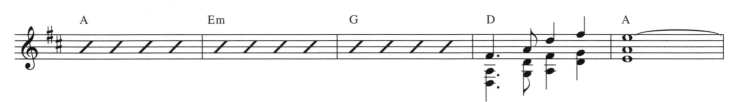

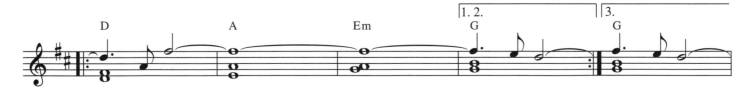

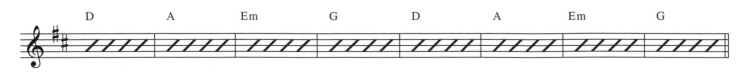

Monroe

Music by Bill Frisell

Good Dog, Happy Man

Music by Bill Frisell

Alternate Bass Line

Poem for Eva

Music by Bill Frisell

Moderately

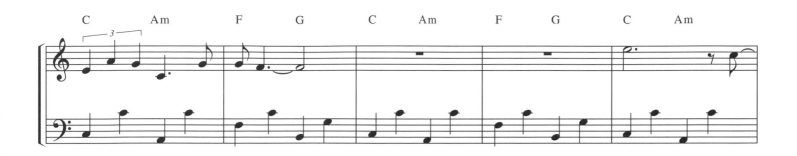

Play 4 times *Repeat and fade*

Rain, Rain

Music by Bill Frisell

What a World

Music by Bill Frisell

Medium tempo

Tell Your Ma, Tell Your Pa

Music by Bill Frisell

Variation on a Theme
(Tales from the Farside)

Music by Bill Frisell

Moderately fast

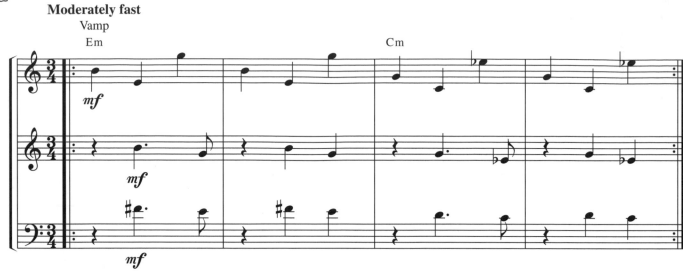

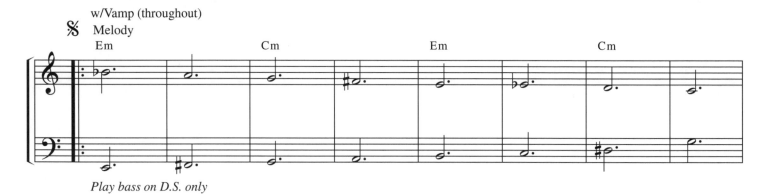

Play bass on D.S. only

To Coda

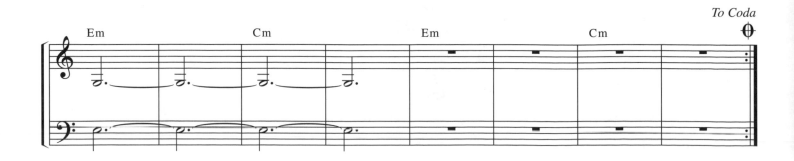

D.S. (no repeat) al Coda

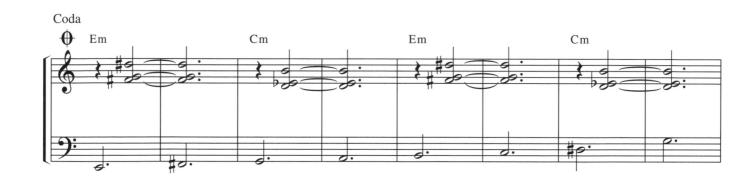

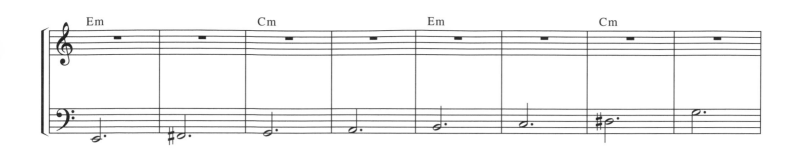

Repeat and fade

Big Bob

Music by Bill Frisell

Medium tempo

Winter Always Turns to Spring

Music by Bill Frisell

Justice and Honor

Music by Bill Frisell

Fingers Snappin' and Toes Tappin'

Music by Bill Frisell

Blues Dream

Music by Bill Frisell

Slowly

Pretty Stars Were Made to Shine

Music by Bill Frisell

Medium tempo

117

Ron Carter

Music by Bill Frisell

Moderately

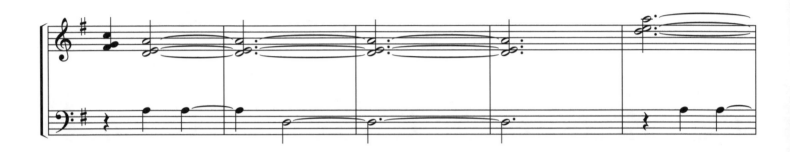

119

Pretty Flowers Were Made for Blooming

Music by Bill Frisell

Where Do We Go?

Music by Bill Frisell

What Do We Do?

Music by Bill Frisell

Dream On

Music by Bill Frisell

TIMELINE

1951
Born in Baltimore, Maryland, March 18. Moved with his parents to Denver, Colorado.

1953
Bill's brother Robert Benjamin was born (June 3).

1955
Built his first guitar out of a piece of cardboard and some rubber bands for strings after being inspired by Jimmy, leader of the Mouseketeers, on the *Mickey Mouse Club* TV series.

1960
Began studying the clarinet. Joined the Gold Sash Band, a marching and concert band he would be involved in for eight years. Studied clarinet privately with Jack Stevens, the band's director. It was here that he learned the fundamentals of music. Also played clarinet in the Teller Elementary School band directed by Jack Fredrickson.

1962
Bill looked up to his older friend George Kawamoto, who lived across the street. George was playing guitar by this time and Bill wanted to also. The first songs he tried to learn were by the Ventures and the Astronauts. Got his first "real guitar" for Christmas—a $20 archtop.

1963
Bought his first record, "Little Deuce Coupe/Surfer Girl," by the Beach Boys, a 45-rpm single. Entered Gove Junior High School. Played in the school band directed by Charles Fields. Began playing tenor saxophone.

1964
Traveled to New York for the first time to perform at the World's Fair with the Gold Sash Band. Saw the Beatles on *The Ed Sullivan Show*. Took some guitar lessons from Bob Marcus at the Denver Folklore Center. This was a fantastic music store, record shop, concert hall, and meeting place for musicians, where he heard about Paul Butterfield, Otis Spann, Junior Wells, Buddy Guy, Elizabeth Cotton, and many others. It was here that he heard Frank Zappa's *Freak Out* album for the first time.

1965
Bought his first electric guitar (Fender Mustang guitar and Deluxe amp) at Happy Logan Music with money earned on a paper route. Went to a Herman's Hermits concert (first live concert). Started first band (the Weeds) with Greg Jones on drums and Tony Eberhart on guitar.

1966
Started going to many more live concerts (Buffalo Springfield, Bob Dylan, Jimi Hendrix, Paul Butterfield, Ravi Shankar, James Brown). Started East High School and continued playing clarinet in the school band directed by Vincent Tagliavore. Other East High students included Philip Bailey, Larry Dunn, and Andrew Wolfolk, who were in a band called the Mellow Mystics. After high school they all went to Los Angeles and joined Earth, Wind & Fire.

1967
Began clarinet studies with Richard Joiner of the Denver Symphony. Learned Wes Montgomery's "Bumpin on Sunset" and performed it at the all school talent shows with Mike Ringler on drums and Bob Chamberlain on bass. This eventually evolved into the Soul Merchants, with Chauncy Blakely or Victor Cooper on vocals, Keary Nitta on tenor sax, Rick Yamamoto on alto sax, and Ken Wright on trumpet. Played songs by James Brown and the Temptations at school dances and fraternity parties. Went to Interlochen Arts Academy for the summer. Went to more concerts—Big Brother and the Holding Company, Sons of Champlin, Electric Flag, Chuck Berry, Canned Heat, Blue Cheer.

1968
Played in the McDonald's All American High School Band at the Rose Bowl parade in Los Angeles and the Thanksgiving Day parade in New York. Went to a Charles Lloyd concert. The band included Keith Jarrett, Ron McClure, and Paul Motian. Heard Gary Burton, Thelonious Monk, Cannonball Adderley, and Dionne Warwick at a jazz festival at Red Rocks Amphitheater.

1969
Began guitar lessons with Dale Bruning, who brought to his attention Charlie Parker, Sonny Rollins, Jim Hall, Bill Evans, Charles Ives, and so many others for the first time. Bruning helped Bill apply many of the theoretical concepts he'd learned on clarinet to the guitar and opened up the whole world of jazz. His parents moved to South Orange, New Jersey, just outside of New York City. Made his first visit to the Village Vanguard where he would eventually hear Charles Mingus, Roland Kirk, Gary Burton, Thad Jones & Mel Lewis, Elvin Jones, Dexter Gordon, Charlie Rouse, Hank Jones, Freddie Hubbard, Sonny Rollins, and Chick Corea. Went to hear Lou Rawls and Al Kooper in Central Park instead of going to Woodstock. Started studies at the University of Northern Colorado as a music major on clarinet. Played tenor saxophone and guitar in the big bands.

1970
With UNC Jazz band went to intercollegiate jazz festivals in Salt Lake City, Utah, and Champaign-Urbana, Illinois. Won outstanding soloist awards at both festivals. Judges included Quincy Jones, Gary Burton, Oliver Nelson, Cannonball Adderley, Benny Carter. Continued studies with Dale Bruning. Also studied with Johnny Smith at UNC. Heard Miles Davis Group with Gary Bartz, Michael Henderson, Jack DeJohnette, Airto, and Keith Jarrett. Played in the group Joshua with other UNC students—Lyle Waller, trombone; John Sherberg, electric piano; Bob Gillis, trumpet; Keary Nitta, saxophone; Fred Hamilton, bass; Alan Aluisi, drums.

1971
Decided to stop playing clarinet and saxophone to concentrate on guitar. Jim Hall came to Denver to play for a week at the Senate Lounge with Bill's teacher Dale Bruning on bass and guitar. Bill met Jim for the first time there. Attended Berklee College of Music in Boston for one semester. Went to the Jazz Workshop and Paul's Mall in Boston for the first time, where he would eventually hear Hubert Laws, Herbie Hancock, Larry Corryell, Jack DeJohnette, Dave Liebman, McCoy Tyner, Anthony Braxton, Sonny Rollins, the Tony Williams Lifetime, Bill Evans, the MJQ, Pat Martino, Ron Carter, Dave Sanborn, B.B. King, James Cotton, Pat Metheny, Stuff, Gary Burton, and others. Heard Jim Hall and Ron Carter duet at the New York City club the Guitar.

1972

Studied for eight weeks with Jim Hall in New York City. Heard Sonny Rollins at the Village Vanguard. Moved back to Colorado and continued studies with Dale Bruning. Played in the Bermuda Brass, a small big band that played Glenn Miller arrangements. The Bill Evans Trio performed for a week at the Senate Lounge—Bill was there almost every night and had the opportunity to meet him. Taught guitar at Gordon Close's Melody Music. One of Bill's students at the time was Kenny Vaughn, a great guitarist now living in Nashville who plays with Lucinda Williams and many others.

1973–74

Continued teaching. Performed jazz gigs around Denver with Bob Gillis and Dale Bruning at places like the Folklore Center, Global Village, and Downstairs Lounge. Recorded a few local commercial jingles, went to jam sessions, and played shows with Rod McKuen and Frank Gorshin. Met and played with Mike Miller, a guitarist who influenced Bill a lot at the time.

1975–77

Returned to Boston and the Berklee College of Music where, on the first day, he met Kermit Driscoll. He also met and played with Tiger Okoshi, Pat Metheny, Mike Stern, Vinnie Johnson, Vinnie Colaiuta, Tommy Campbell, Leni Stern, Joe Lovano, Hank Roberts, Lowell Davidson, Donald Rubinstein. Studied jazz guitar with John Damian and arranging and composition with Mike Gibbs and Herb Pomeroy. Played in a top-40 band, the Boston Connection, with Kermit Driscoll and Vinnie Colaiuta. Played often at Michael's and Pooh's Pub. Heard Michael Gregory Jackson, whose way of playing would prove very influential.

1978

Moved to Belgium to play in a band with Steve Houben, Greg Badolato, Vinnie Johnson, and Kermit Driscoll, resulting in first record, *Mauve Traffic*. Began writing his own music. Met Carole D'Inverno who he would marry one year later. Heard Ornette Coleman at the North Sea Jazz Festival. On two separate occasions during the festival Ornette approached Bill and asked, "Where did you get that Coke?" and "What's back here?" Toured England with the Mike Gibbs Orchestra, which included Charlie Mariano, Kenny Wheeler, and Eberhard Weber. Played on Eberhard Weber's *Fluid Rustle* with Gary Burton for ECM. This is where Bill first met Manfred Eicher.

1979–80

Moved to New Jersey/New York City area. Met and played with D. Sharpe, Bob Moses, Percy Jones, Mike Clark, Dave Samuels, Julius Hemphill, Billy Drewes, Tom Rainey, Scott Lee, Ratzo Harris, and Nick Pike. Played club dates, weddings. Played with Men Working, with Alan Brower. Recorded with Chet Baker in Belgium. Played at the New York clubs 7th Avenue South and 55 Grand Street.

1981

On Pat Metheny's recommendation, Bill played with Paul Motian for the first time. Toured Europe as a duo with Eberhard Weber. Met Thomas Stöwsand, who worked at ECM at the time and is now Bill's European agent. At ECM he also met Hans Wendl, who later worked as Bill's manager and now handles his publishing. First European tour with Paul Motian and recording of Motian's album *Psalm* for ECM. Also recorded *Paths, Prints* with Jan Garbarek. Recorded a track on *Amarcord Nino Rota*, his first recording under his own name and first of many collaborations with producer Hal Willner.

1982

Recorded *In Line* for ECM, his first album under his own name. Met John Zorn at the Soho Music Gallery where he was working at the time.

1983

Met Bob Hurwitz who worked for ECM in New York. Bob would later take over Nonesuch Records.

1984

Recorded *Rambler*. Toured with Julius Hemphill.

1985

Daughter Monica Jane was born.

1986

Played duet concert with Jim Hall at Walker Art Center in Minneapolis. Started the first band under his own name with Kermit Driscoll, Joey Baron, and Hank Roberts. Recorded *Lookout for Hope*, his first band record and first time he worked with Lee Townsend as producer. Lee is now Bill's manager.

1987

Left ECM and began present relationship with Nonesuch Records. Performed at the Knitting Factory in New York playing the music of Robin Holcomb with Doug Wieselman and John Zorn's composition "Hu Die" with Fred Frith and Ruby Chang during the Knitting Factory's first series of concerts.

1988

Bill's friend, Betty Berkin, gave him a John Hiatt record, *Bring the Family*, with Jim Keltner, Ry Cooder, and Nick Lowe. He became a big fan of all these guys.

1989

Recorded *Is That You?* with Wayne Horvitz as producer for the first time. Moved with his family to Seattle.

Since 1989

Since 1989 Bill's work has been very well documented on his many recordings. His performance schedule has been more and more taken up with his own projects. He continues to play with the Paul Motian Trio with Joe Lovano and has also performed with Jim Hall, Don Byron, Ginger Baker, Charlie Haden, David Sanborn, Marianne Faithful, Elvis Costello, Ron Carter, and the Hal Willner–produced tribute to Harry Smith. He performed Steve Mackey's "Deal" at Carnegie Hall with the American Composers Orchestra conducted by Dennis Russell Davies and in Los Angeles with members of the L.A. Philharmonic conducted by Essa Pecka Salonen. As he is also becoming more active as a film composer, Bill's music can be heard in Gary Larson's *Tales from the Farside*, Gus Van Sant's *Psycho* and *Finding Forrester*, Rory Kennedy's HBO documentary *American Hollow*, and Wim Wenders's *Million Dollar Hotel* (with Brian Blade, Jon Hassell, Bono, Daniel Lanois, Brian Eno, Greg Cohen, and Adam Dorn). He has also written music for the Frankfurt Ballett and the ACT Theatre's production of *Temporary Help*. He has been featured on TV on *Night Music*, *The Tonight Show with Jay Leno*, and *Sessions at West 54th Street*.

When he's home, he likes to play at clubs like the Tractor Tavern and the OK Hotel. He continues to work with Wayne Horvitz and Robin Holcomb, and it was in the Northwest that he had the opportunity to meet many musicians and artists who have been an inspiration— Eyvind Kang, Michael Shrieve, Danny Barnes, Keith Lowe, Christos Govetas, Martin Hayes, Boubakar Traore, Sidiki Camara, the film director Gus Van Sant, cartoonists Jim Woodring and Gary Larson, the painter Claude Utley, and so many others.

SELECTED DISCOGRAPHY

WITH DAVE HOLLAND & ELVIN JONES
with Dave Holland, bass; Elvin Jones, drums
Nonesuch, 2001

BLUES DREAM
with Greg Leisz, slide guitars & mandolin;
David Piltch, bass; Kenny Wollesen, drums;
Ron Miles, trumpet; Curtis Fowlkes, trombone;
Billy Drewes, alto saxophone
Nonesuch, 2001

GHOST TOWN
Solo (Bill Frisell, guitars, banjo & bass)
Nonesuch, 2000

THE SWEETEST PUNCH
The New Songs of Elvis Costello and Burt Bacharach,
arranged by Bill Frisell
with Don Byron, clarinets; Billy Drewes, alto saxophone;
Ron Miles, trumpet; Curtis Fowlkes, trombone;
Viktor Krauss, bass; Brian Blade, drums
Decca, 1999

GOOD DOG, HAPPY MAN
with Greg Leisz, slide guitars & mandolin;
Wayne Horvitz, organ; Viktor Krauss, bass;
Jim Keltner, drums; Ry Cooder, guitar
Nonesuch, 1999

GONE, JUST LIKE A TRAIN
with Viktor Krauss, bass; Jim Keltner, drums
Nonesuch, 1998

NASHVILLE
with Viktor Krauss, bass; Jerry Douglas, dobro;
Ron Block, banjo & guitar; Adam Steffey, mandolin;
Robin Holcomb, vocal; Pat Bergeson, harmonica
Nonesuch, 1997

QUARTET
with Eyvind Kang, violin; Ron Miles, trumpet;
Curtis Fowlkes, trombone
Nonesuch, 1996

LIVE
with Kermit Driscoll, bass; Joey Baron, drums
Rykodisc/Gramavision, 1995

THE HIGH SIGN & ONE WEEK
Music for the Films of Buster Keaton
with Kermit Driscoll, bass; Joey Baron, drums
Nonesuch, 1995

GO WEST
Music for the Films of Buster Keaton
with Kermit Driscoll, bass; Joey Baron, drums
Nonesuch, 1995

THIS LAND
with Kermit Driscoll, bass; Joey Baron, drums;
Don Byron, clarinets; Billy Drewes, alto saxophone;
Curtis Fowlkes, trombone
Nonesuch, 1994

HAVE A LITTLE FAITH
with Don Byron, clarinets; Guy Klucevsek, accordion;
Kermit Driscoll, bass; Joey Baron, drums
Nonesuch, 1993

WHERE IN THE WORLD?
with Hank Roberts, cello; Kermit Driscoll, bass;
Joey Baron, drums
Elektra Musician/Nonesuch, 1991

IS THAT YOU?
with Wayne Horvitz, keyboards; Joey Baron, drums;
Dave Hofstra, tuba & bass
Elektra Musician/Nonesuch, 1990

BEFORE WE WERE BORN
with Hank Roberts, cello; Kermit Driscoll, bass;
Joey Baron, drums; Julius Hemphill, alto saxophone;
Billy Drewes, alto saxophone; Arto Lindsay, guitar & voice;
Peter Scherer, keyboards; Cyro Baptista, percussion
Elektra Musician/Nonesuch, 1989

LOOKOUT FOR HOPE
with Hank Roberts, cello; Kermit Driscoll, bass;
Joey Baron, drums
ECM, 1987

RAMBLER
with Kenny Wheeler, trumpet & flügelhorn; Bob Stewart,
tuba; Jerome Harris, bass; Paul Motian, drums
ECM, 1985

IN LINE
Solo & Duo; with Arild Andersen, bass
ECM, 1983

Songs also recorded with lyrics:
Throughout (appears as "Steady, Girl"):
Lyrics and vocals by Arto Lindsay, on *Before We Were Born*, Nonesuch
Deep Dead Blue:
Lyrics and vocals by Elvis Costello, on Elvis Costello/Bill Frisell:
Deep Dead Blue, Warner Bros.
Gone, Just Like a Train:
Lyrics and vocals by Victor Bruce Godsey, on Bill Frisell/Victor Bruce
Godsey/Brian Ales: *American Blood/Safety by Numbers*,
Intuition Records
Rambler ("Tren de la Medianoche/Rambler"),
When We Go ("Cuando Me Vaya"):
Lyrics and vocals (in Spanish) by Gabriela, on Gabriela: *Detras del Sol*,
Intuition Records
Family ("Ecos de Allá Atrás"),
Lonesome ("Una Luz en la Ventana"),
The Way Home ("El Camino a Casa"):
Lyrics and vocals (in Spanish) by Gabriela, on Gabriela: *Viento Rojo*,
Intuition Records
Gimme a Holler:
Lyrics and vocals by Akiko Yano, on Akiko Yano: *Go Girl*,
Epic Records

INDEX

1951 18	Mr. Memory 75
Again 48	Music I Heard 8
Amarillo Barbados 15	My Buffalo Girl 97
Bacon Bunch, The 71	Nature's Symphony 89
Beautiful E 46	Pioneers, The 100
Big Bob 112	Pip Squeak 26
Big Shoe 96	Pleased to Meet You 88
Blues Dream 117	Poem for Eva 105
Blues for Los Angeles 84	Pretty Flowers Were Made for Blooming 120
Brother 76	Pretty Stars Were Made to Shine 117
Cadillac 1959 98	Rag 32
Child at Heart 44	Rain, Rain 106
Coffaro's Theme 73	Rambler 9
Cold, Cold Ground 101	Resistor 10
Deep Dead Blue 66	Rob Roy 42
Dream On 123	Ron Carter 118
Egg Radio 70	Roscoe 95
Family (Version 1) 79	Sherlock, Jr. 92
Family (Version 2) 80	Stand Up, Sit Down 65
Fingers Snappin' and Toes Tappin' 116	Strange Meeting (Version 1) 12
Freddy's Step 24	Strange Meeting (Version 2) 56
Gallows, The 72	Tales from the Farside 68
Gimme a Holler 74	Tell Your Ma, Tell Your Pa 108
Girl Asks Boy, Part 1 86	That Was Then 102
Gone, Just Like a Train 93	This Land 57
Good Dog, Happy Man 104	Throughout (Version 1) 6
Goodbye 27	Throughout (Version 2) 7
Hangdog 20	Twenty Years 34
Hard Plains Drifter 28	Unscientific Americans 16
Hello Nellie 38	Unsung Heroes 40
Hope and Fear 37	Variation on a Theme (Tales from the Farside) 110
Jimmy Carter, Part 1 58	Verona 83
Jimmy Carter, Part 2 60	Way Home, The 33
Julius Hemphill 64	We're Not from Around Here 82
Justice and Honor 115	What a World 107
Keep Your Eyes Open 78	What Do We Do? 122
Let Me In 53	When We Go 14
Lonesome 22	Where Do We Go? 121
Lookout for Hope 17	Where in the World? 50
Monica Jane 63	Wife and Kid, The 94
Monroe 103	Winter Always Turns to Spring 114

Guitar one™

The Magazine You Can Play

Visit the Guitar One web site at www.guitarone.com

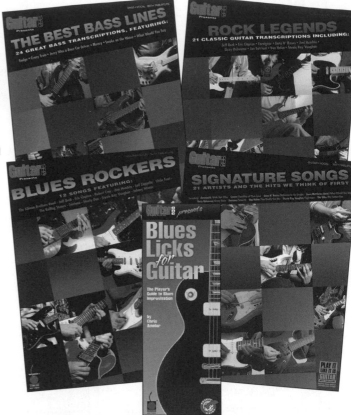

GuitarOne Presents · The Best Bass Lines

INCLUDES TAB

Get the low-down on the low-end sounds from 24 super songs, straight from the pages of *GuitarOne* magazine! Includes note-for-note bass transcriptions with tab for: Badge • Bohemian Rhapsody • Celebrity Skin • Crash into Me • Crazy Train • Everything Zen • Glycerine • Jerry Was a Race Car Driver • Money • November Rain • Smoke on the Water • Suffragette City • Sweet Child O' Mine • Violet • What Would You Say • You're My Flavor • and more.

_____02500311 Play-It-Like-It-Is Bass $14.95

GuitarOne Presents · Blues Licks for Guitar · *by Chris Amelar*

A great guide to blues improvisation that will fit in your guitar case! This book will help you develop a strong blues vocabulary by teaching many of the licks and phrases essential to playing blues solos. Also examines scales used in blues improv, and techniques like bending and vibrato. Includes an intro by guitar pro Chris Amelar, and a complete 12-bar blues solo at the end of the book. 4½" x 12"

_____02500118...$5.95

GuitarOne Presents · Blues Rockers

INCLUDES TAB

12 rockin' blues favorites, including: Changes • I Can't Quit You Baby • Jingo (Jin-Go-Lo-Ba) • Ramblin' Man • Smoking Gun • Steppin' Out • Tightrope • and more.

_____02500264 Play-It-Like-It-Is Guitar $14.95

GuitarOne Presents · Legends of Lead Guitar

The Best of Interviews: 1995-2000

Who can explain the extensive thought processes and flights of fancy by which a virtuoso guitarist makes a metal, wood & wire contraption sing, snarl, whisper or weep? None but the artist. Hence this book. *Legends of Lead Guitar* is a fascinating compilation of *GuitarOne* magazine interviews with today's greatest lead guitarists – and your backstage pass to the art of the rock'n'roll axe! From deeply rooted blues giants to the most fearless pioneer, legendary players reveal how they achieve their extraordinary craft. Artists featured include: AC/DC • Aerosmith • Jeff Beck • Black Crowes • Bush • Coal Chamber • Collective Soul • Creed • Deftones • Ani DiFranco • Kevin Eubanks • Foo Fighters • Goo Goo Dolls • Buddy Guy • Eric Johnson • Kid Rock • B.B. King • Kiss • Korn • Lenny Kravitz • Limp Bizkit • Metallica • Dave Navarro • Jimmy Page • Pantera • Les Paul • Rage Against the Machine • Red Hot Chili Peppers • Carlos Santana • Kenny Wayne Shepherd • Andy Summers • Third Eye Blind • Steve Vai • Eddie Van Halen • and more!

_____02500329 ....$19.95

GuitarOne Presents · Lesson Lab

This exceptional book/CD pack features more than 20 in-depth lessons from the pages of *GuitarOne* magazine's most popular department. Tackle a variety of pertinent music- and guitar-related subjects, such as scales, chords, theory, guitar technique, songwriting, and much more!

_____02500330 Book/CD Pack..$19.95

GuitarOne Presents · Noise and Feedback

_____02500328 ....$16.95

GuitarOne Presents · Rock Legends

INCLUDES TAB

Transcriptions with tab for 21 rock classics from some of the greatest guitarists ever! Includes: All Along the Watchtower (Hendrix) • Badge (Cream) • Crazy on You (Heart) • Crazy Train (Osbourne) • Flying in a Blue Dream (Satriani) • Hide Away (Clapton) • Hot Blooded (Foreigner) • Sweet Child O' Mine (Guns N' Roses) • Telephone Song (Stevie Ray Vaughan) • You Really Got Me (Van Halen) • and more.

_____02500262 Play-It-Like-It-Is Guitar...$14.95

GuitarOne Presents · Signature Songs

INCLUDES TAB

This cool collection features 21 artists and note-for-note transcriptions of the hit songs that remind us of them! Includes: Aerosmith, "Walk This Way" • Cream, "Sunshine of Your Love" • Guns N' Roses, "Welcome to the Jungle" • Dave Matthews Band, "What Would You Say" • Ozzy Osbourne, "Crazy Train" • Santana, "Smooth" • Van Halen, "You Really Got Me" • The Who, "My Generation" • and more!

_____02500303 Play-It-Like-It-Is Guitar..$16.95

GuitarOne Presents · Studio City · *by Carl Verheyen*

Professional guitarist Carl Verheyen chronicles his career as one of L.A.'s top-call session players in this complete collection of his Studio City columns from *Guitar* magazine. He draws on his vast experience to advise guitarists how to: exercise studio etiquette and act professionally • acquire, assemble and set up gear for sessions • use the tricks of the trade to become a studio hero • get repeat callbacks • and much more. This is the handbook for recording guitarists who want a career as a professional studio player!

_____02500195 ....$9.95

Prices, contents, and availability subject to change without notice.

Visit Cherry Lane Online at **www.cherrylane.com**